ISBN: 9781099492167

WRitteN aND iLLUStRateD BY DiaNe HaMeLe-BeNa

Life eNHaNCeR PUBLiCatiONS

NeW YORK, USA

www.lifeenhancer.expert

FiRSt PRiNtiNG eDitiON 2019

DEDICATED TO OUR MOTHER AND FATHER,
WHO TAUGHT US HOW TO HAVE FUN.

CIRCLE AT LEAST 11 DIFFERENCES BETWEEN THESE TWO DRAWINGS.

PUZZLE 1 CLUES

ACROSS	
6	LARGE, COLORFUL MOVIE SIGN
7	EMBRACE; TO WRAP YOUR ARMS AROUND SOMEONE
8	FRIVOLITY
9	CHOIR MEMBER
11	ROOSTER'S MATE
12	NOT HAPPY
17	FATHER'S MATE
19	NOT IN
20	FISHERMAN'S TOOL USED TO SCOOP UP FISH
21	DOVE IS MAKING THIS SOUND

DOWN	
1	MORNING BEVERAGE
2	OPPOSITE OF SIT
3	PUT ON CLOTHES
4	EXPRESS APPRECIATION TO SOMEONE
5	MONSTER
10	SANTA'S HAT COLOR
11	MEAT EATEN WITH EGGS
13	HUMPHREY BOGART'S SKILL
14	US FLAG COLOR
15	ABANDONED, DEMOLISHED SHIP
16	ENGINE
18	PIG SOUND

CROSSWORD PUZZLE 1

MAKE THIS INTO A FRUIT TREE.

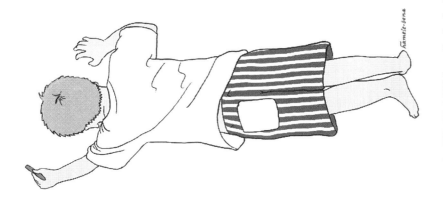

DRAW SOME GRAFFITI ON THE WALL.
INCLUDE WORDS AND IMAGES THAT EXPRESS HOW YOU ARE FEELING.

CARS

```
I  Q  H  W  A  G  O  N  H  F  U  S
N  C  H  E  V  Y  E  N  B  O  P  E
Y  X  J  B  U  I  C  K  F  R  W  D
W  J  A  G  U  A  R  I  M  D  G  A
P  N  H  Y  P  A  C  K  A  R  D  N
C  A  D  I  L  L  A  C  T  O  Y  W
M  E  R  C  E  D  E  S  C  N  C  X
I  B  M  W  V  E  A  U  G  U  H  U
```

CIRCLE THE FOLLOWING WORDS.
WORDS ARE HIDDEN ➤ AND ▼

BMW

BUICK

CADILLAC

CHEVY

FORD

JAGUAR

MERCEDES

PACKARD

SEDAN

WAGON

HELP THIS LITTLE GIRL MAKE A DESIGN ON THE WALL.

FINISH DRAWING THIS CAR, AND THEN COLOR IT.

THESE BIRDS ARE CALLED LINNIES.
MAKE THEM COLORFUL AND NAME THEM.

COLOR THE BACKGROUND.
IS THERE A SUN? A MOON? STARS? TREES?

COLORS

```
O  W  L  B  L  U  E  R  E  D  A  T
R  O  Y  E  L  L  O  W  H  R  T  X
A  P  E  R  I  W  I  N  K  L  E  W
N  U  H  A  B  L  A  C  K  H  T  H
G  T  T  E  P  U  R  P  L  E  V  I
E  R  J  I  B  Q  P  I  N  K  K  T
V  C  G  R  E  E  N  P  A  D  D  E
Y  N  M  G  J  V  Q  J  H  L  H  U
```

CIRCLE THE FOLLOWING WORDS.
WORDS ARE HIDDEN ➡ AND ⬇

BLACK   PERIWINKLE   WHITE
BLUE   PINK   YELLOW
GREEN   PURPLE
ORANGE   RED

DRAW A BODY FOR THIS KING.
WHAT IS HIS STORY?

ANIMALS

WRITE A WORD IN THE NEXT BUBBLE. THE WORD
SHOULD BE AN ANIMAL WORD THAT BEGINS WITH
THE LAST LETTER OF THE WORD BEFORE IT!

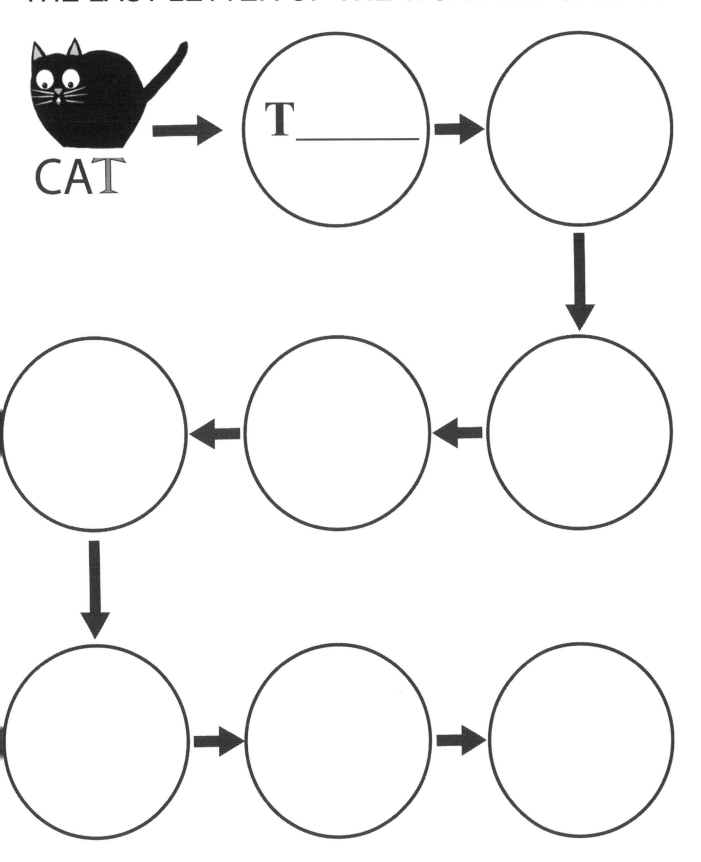

CAT

T_____

PUZZLE 2 CLUES

ACROSS

6	MOTHER'S MATE
7	LET FALL
8	TREE PRODUCT USED TO MAKE FURNITURE
9	FIT TO BE EATEN
10	A BUSYBODY IS THIS
12	TO PUT IN THE MAIL/POST
15	PHYSICALLY FULL OF ENERGY
17	MUSICAL NUMBER
18	BATS LIVE IN THIS
19	METALLIC ELEMENT USED TO MAKE MIRRORS

DOWN

1	DARK BROWNISH-RED COLOR
2	DULL SOUND OF HEAVY ITEM FALLING
3	ATTEMPTS
4	LOOK UP TO A HERO
5	HAMMER OR WRENCH, FOR EXAMPLE
11	THIN SLICE OF PIE
13	DID THE FOXTROT
14	INGREDIENT USED TO MAKE BEER AND BREAD
16	APPLAUD
17	ROUND TOWER ON A FARM FOR STORING GRAIN FOR COWS

CROSSWORD PUZZLE 2

—

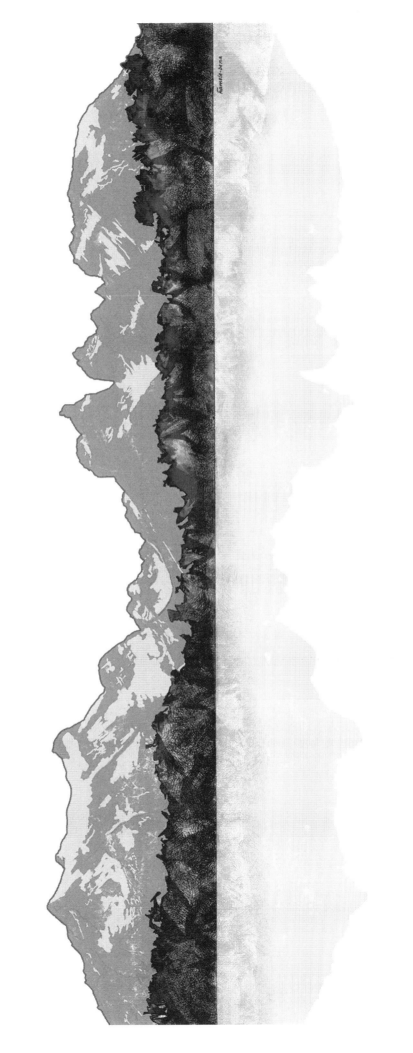

MAKE A SUNSET. ADD A FLYING SAUCER!

–

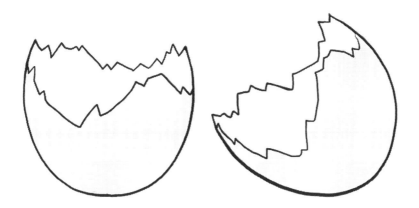

DRAW WHAT HATCHED OUT OF THIS EGG.

FIREFIGHTER

J	L	M	M	N	P	A	V	E	L	Y	E
C	H	O	S	E	F	P	W	N	A	L	C
H	Y	D	R	A	N	T	A	G	D	N	H
V	Q	A	L	A	R	M	T	I	D	D	I
O	Z	H	Z	Z	C	P	E	N	E	A	E
T	J	Y	A	N	V	Q	R	E	R	T	F
W	R	T	F	L	A	M	E	S	H	T	B
X	B	O	O	T	S	S	M	O	K	E	A

CIRCLE THE FOLLOWING WORDS.
WORDS ARE HIDDEN → AND ↓

ALARM
BOOTS
CHIEF
ENGINE
FLAMES
HOSE
HYDRANT
LADDER

SMOKE
WATER

DRAW A MOVIE STAR FACE AND A HAT.

FOOD

WRITE A WORD IN THE NEXT BUBBLE. THE WORD
SHOULD BE A FOOD WORD THAT BEGINS WITH
THE LAST LETTER OF THE WORD BEFORE IT!

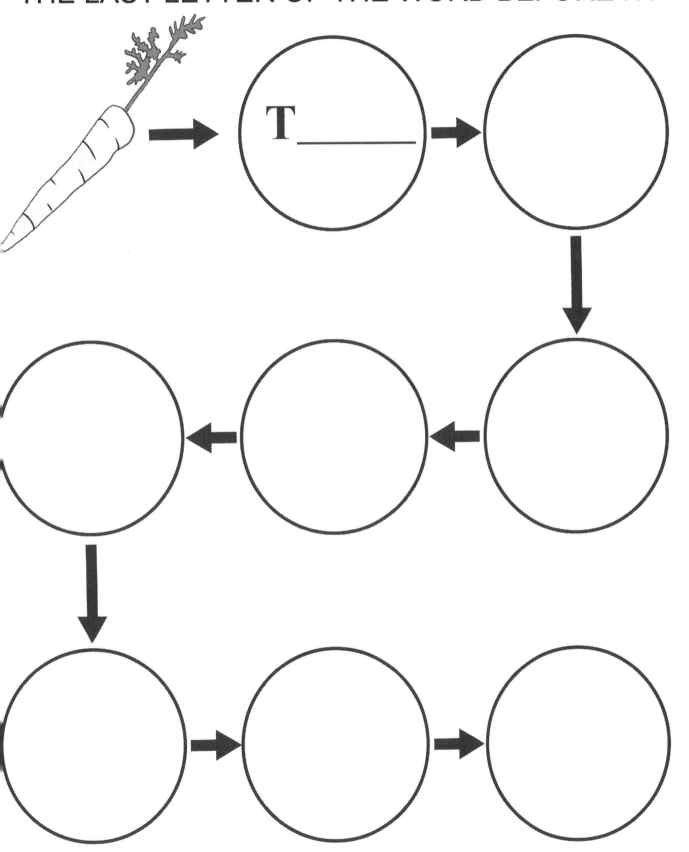

T_____

MAKE US COLORFUL!

PUZZLE 3 CLUES

ACROSS

1	NOISY SLEEP SOUND
3	THIN SOUP MADE FROM MEAT OR VEGETABLES
6	COLLECTION OF RAIN ON SIDEWALK
8	UNABLE TO HEAR
10	A PARAKEET BEGINS LIFE IN THIS
11	SMALL, CHEWY, CHOCOLATE CAKE-LIKE COOKIE
13	TWO-WHEELED VEHICLE
16	A WRITTEN RULE
17	SITS ATOP A HOUSE
18	GLOBULE OF GAS; YOU CAN MAKE ONE WITH CHEWING GUM
20	SLACKS
21	CHAIR WITH NO ARMS OR BACK

DOWN

1	NINTH MONTH
2	US FLAG COLOR
4	SEA
5	TO BE AFRAID OF SOMETHING
7	GOPHERS AND CHIPMUNKS DO THIS
9	TO COAST WITH TIRES DISENGAGED FROM DRIVING MECHANISM
11	BRITISH BROADCASTING CORPORATION (ABBREVIATION)
12	SINGLE
14	KING'S HAT
15	FLOPPY EAR PART
16	CHEMIST'S HOME
19	WAGER

CROSSWORD PUZZLE 3

MAKE US COLORFUL!

MATCH THE WORDS TO THE FACE.

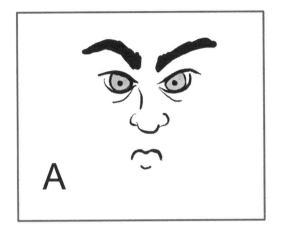

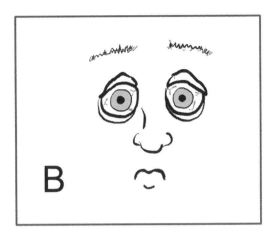

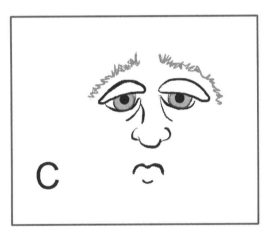

MATCH THE FACE WITH THE STORY.

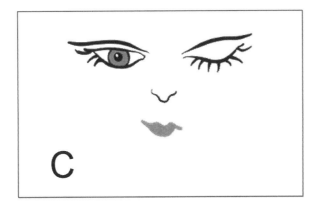

I think they forgot my birthday....
1

Hey, handsome!
2

3
Do you really expect me to finish this work by myself?

—

LINK THE EXPRESSION TO THE SENTIMENT.

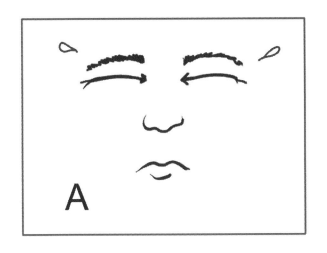

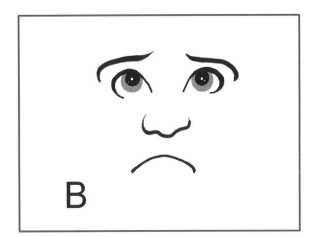

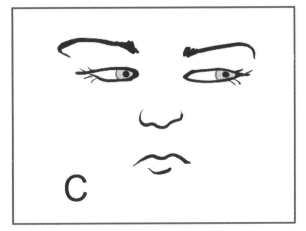

1 I think she's making fun of my bald head....

2 "STRIKE *TWO!*"

3 If she thinks she's going to cut this line and get in front of me, she's crazy....

FOODS

```
C I Z I C E C R E A M U
A L A S A G N A Z M G U
K T C H O C O L A T E C
E C J N E N P I Z Z A P
H A M B U R G E R W C I
A C H I C K E N C S M E
G M P U D D I N G H O I
U S P A G H E T T I R D
```

CIRCLE THE FOLLOWING WORDS.
WORDS ARE HIDDEN ➡ AND ⬇

CAKE

LASAGNA

HAMBURGER

ICE CREAM

PUDDING

PIE

PIZZA

CHOCOLATE

NEXT TO EACH HAT ON THE LEFT,
WRITE THE LETTER OF THE MATCHING ITEM ON THE RIGHT.

DRAW FACES AND FINS FOR THESE FISH.

ICE CREAM

```
Z  I  H  A  Z  E  L  N  U  T  C  T
X  V  A  N  I  L  L  A  I  W  J  A
X  S  T  R  A  W  B  E  R  R  Y  L
W  E  C  H  O  C  O  L  A  T  E  M
M  B  A  N  A  N  A  H  U  C  Y  O
C  O  C  O  N  U  T  R  N  O  L  N
B  U  T  T  E  R  P  E  C  A  N  D
E  P  I  S  T  A  C  H  I  O  C  K
```

CIRCLE THE FOLLOWING WORDS.
WORDS ARE HIDDEN ➜ AND ⬇

ALMOND   COCONUT   VANILLA
BANANA   HAZELNUT
BUTTER PECAN   PISTACHIO
CHOCOLATE   STRAWBERRY

DRAW A BED, TOY, AND FOOD FOR THS PUPPY.

PUZZLE 4 CLUES

ACROSS	
1	WINE FRUIT
4	SOMETHING STUDENTS ATTEND
7	PERIOD OF TEMPORARY ECONOMIC DECLINE
8	OPPOSITE OF BEGINNING
9	BASEBALL PITCH DELIVERED WITH A SPIN: _____ BALL
11	SAD EYES PRODUCE THESE
14	JOE DIMAGGIO USED THIS
17	OPPOSITE OF INTROVERT
18	ABBREVIATED TERM FOR HOMERUN
19	THE BIRD THAT GETS THE WORM
DOWN	
1	FLAVORFUL BULB USED IN ITALIAN FOOD
2	HOLDS A BOAT IN PLACE
3	OPPOSITE OF DIFFICULT
4	CUSTOMER
5	GIRL'S NAME
6	PLANT EMBRYO
10	ONE WHO REVISES NEWSPAPER STORIES
12	SUDDENLY BECOME VISIBLE
13	DALMATIAN DESCRIPTION
14	ALTERNATIVE TO A SHOWER
15	YANKEES OR METS
16	COOING BIRD

CROSSWORD PUZZLE 4

MAKE THIS INTO A TREE IN SUMMER.

MOVIE STARS

```
V  G  B  F  E  C  O  F  B  T  S  B
N  A  R  E  I  O  J  U  D  R  T  F
C  R  A  W  F  O  R  D  G  A  E  O
P  L  N  A  N  P  G  P  A  C  W  N
E  A  D  Y  S  E  C  L  B  Y  A  D
C  N  O  N  Y  R  S  N  L  W  R  A
K  D  Q  E  C  A  G  N  E  Y  T  H
A  S  I  Q  H  E  P  B  U  R  N  H
```

CIRCLE THE FOLLOWING WORDS.
WORDS ARE HIDDEN ➡ AND ⬇

BRANDO   GABLE   TRACY

CAGNEY   GARLAND   WAYNE

COOPER   HEPBURN

CRAWFORD   PECK

FONDA   STEWART

•

DRAW A FEW BOATS, BIRDS, AND A FACE ON THE SUN.

—

THIS IS BARBIE. SHE IS AT THE BEACH. DRAW THE SUN AND OCEAN. GIVE BARBIE A HAT AND SUNGLASSES!

MUSICAL INSTRUMENTS

```
G  F  D  R  U  M  H  K  W  Q  E  H
O  I  D  E  X  F  L  U  T  E  W  P
R  E  B  A  S  S  K  T  Z  B  U  I
G  N  Q  C  L  A  R  I  N  E  T  A
A  K  H  A  R  M  O  N  I  C  A  N
N  M  G  S  T  R  U  M  P  E  T  O
M  G  U  I  T  A  R  U  B  L  G  Z
Q  U  U  B  H  A  R  P  T  M  M  C
```

CIRCLE THE FOLLOWING WORDS.
WORDS ARE HIDDEN ➔ AND ▼

BASS   GUITAR   PIANO
CLARINET   HARMONICA   TRUMPET
DRUM   HARP
FLUTE   ORGAN

MAKE THIS INTO A TREE IN AUTUMN.

DRAW SOMETHING THAT YOU LIKE.

DRAW SOMETHING THAT YOU DON'T LIKE.

—

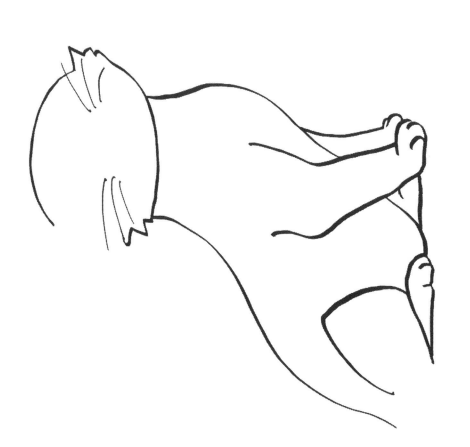

DRAW A FACE AND TAIL FOR MOM CAT.
DRAW FOOD FOR THEM, TOO!

PRESENTS

O	B	A	M	A	W	W	F	Z	S	D	C
D	R	D	Q	J	O	H	N	S	O	N	L
Z	Q	D	S	E	K	B	U	S	H	M	I
E	I	S	E	N	H	O	W	E	R	H	N
T	I	F	O	R	D	N	T	O	P	R	T
C	A	R	T	E	R	N	I	X	O	N	O
P	F	R	E	A	G	A	N	Y	N	O	N
O	W	O	L	K	E	N	N	E	D	Y	Z

CIRCLE THE FOLLOWING WORDS.
WORDS ARE HIDDEN ➡ AND ⬇

BUSH	FORD	OBAMA
CARTER	JOHNSON	REAGAN
CLINTON	KENNEDY	
EISENHOWER	NIXON	

—

DRAW THE OWNER OF THIS BICYCLE AND
ADD SOME OTHER THINGS TO THIS SCENE.

SPRING

```
Z  F  U  W  V  P  O  L  Y  M  R  I
Z  L  I  S  S  B  R  E  E  Z  Y  W
R  O  B  B  J  D  F  A  B  L  O  W
A  W  U  T  H  A  W  V  I  D  G  W
I  E  D  S  L  K  L  E  Y  M  C  A
N  R  S  L  I  F  E  S  J  A  S  R
Z  S  R  C  R  G  R  E  E  N  V  M
M  B  J  C  E  A  S  T  E  R  I  P
```

CIRCLE THE FOLLOWING WORDS.
WORDS ARE HIDDEN ➡ AND ⬇

BREEZY   GREEN   THAW
BUDS   LEAVES   WARM
EASTER   LIFE
FLOWERS   RAIN

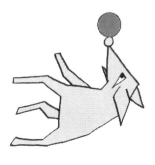

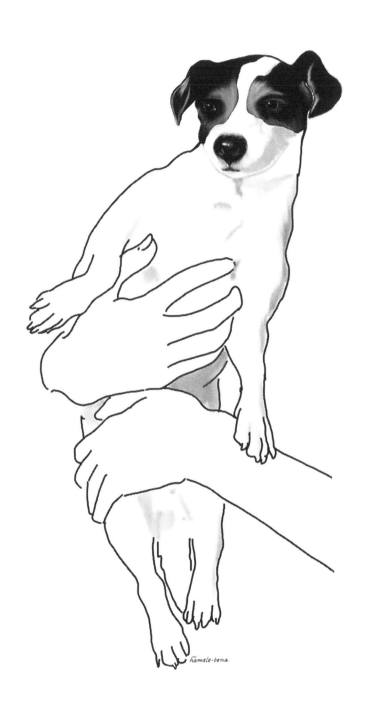

DRAW A BACKGROUND FOR THIS PUPPY.

RELIGION

```
P  C  L  X  C  H  U  R  C  H  R  M
R  L  A  L  T  A  R  X  X  O  E  I
E  E  W  O  R  S  H  I  P  Q  V  N
A  R  S  A  C  R  E  D  E  A  E  I
C  G  A  R  Q  P  R  A  Y  E  R  S
H  Y  M  N  I  P  E  W  B  K  E  T
C  R  A  B  B  I  B  S  V  Y  N  E
T  E  M  P  L  E  I  N  A  H  D  R
```

CIRCLE THE FOLLOWING WORDS.
WORDS ARE HIDDEN ➤ AND ▼

ALTAR	PEW	SACRED
CHURCH	PRAYER	TEMPLE
CLERGY	PREACH	WORSHIP
HYMN	RABBI	
MINISTER	REVEREND	

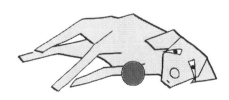

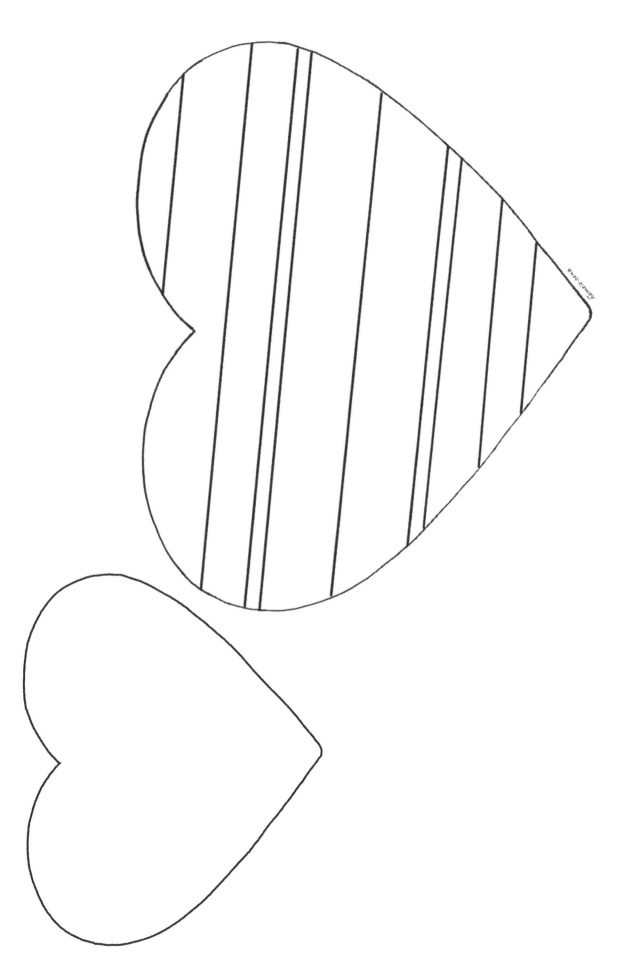

COLOR THESE HEARTS WITH THE COLORS YOU LIKE!

CIRCLE 4 THAT ARE DIFFERENT.

DRAW YOURSELF.

BOOZE

```
Z  Z  X  A  B  W  B  T  Y  S  D  Y
K  V  I  X  O  H  R  E  N  C  I  N
T  O  U  R  U  I  A  Q  H  O  M  B
A  D  R  W  R  S  N  U  Q  T  O  E
G  K  U  I  B  K  D  I  W  C  V  E
I  A  M  N  O  E  Y  L  M  H  Q  R
N  P  P  E  N  Y  L  A  V  E  K  H
K  Y  Y  P  P  C  O  G  N  A  C  O
```

CIRCLE THE FOLLOWING WORDS.
WORDS ARE HIDDEN ➡ AND ⬇

BEER	GIN	TEQUILA
BOURBON	RUM	VODKA
BRANDY	SCOTCH	WHISKEY
COGNAC		WINE

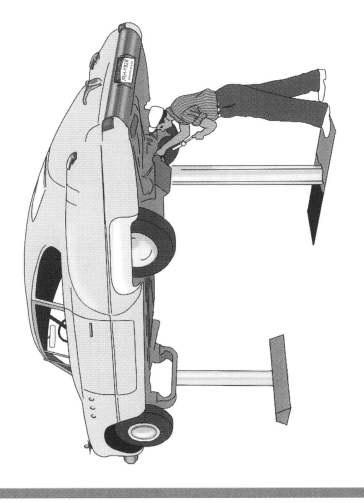

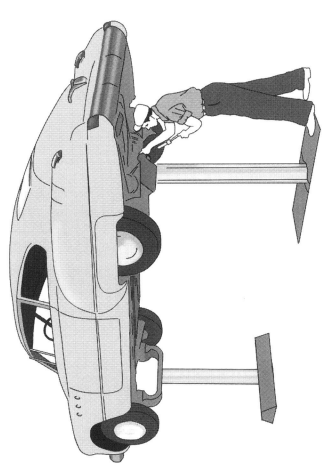

CIRCLE 10 DIFFERENCES BETWEEN THESE TWO DRAWINGS.

THE FLU

```
F  L  U  I  D  S  J  I  I  T  S  S
V  I  T  A  M  I  N  D  A  S  L  N
C  O  A  C  H  E  S  I  N  B  E  E
R  E  S  T  D  O  C  T  O  R  E  E
P  T  I  S  S  U  E  E  S  V  P  Z
D  V  A  P  O  R  I  Z  E  R  D  E
T  H  E  R  M  O  M  E  T  E  R  E
C  O  U  G  H  O  Y  W  O  Z  H  J
```

CIRCLE THE FOLLOWING WORDS.
WORDS ARE HIDDEN ➡ AND ⬇

ACHES   REST   TISSUE
COUGH   SLEEP   VAPORIZER
DOCTOR   SNEEZE   VITAMIN D
FLUIDS   THERMOMETER

PUZZLE 5 CLUES

ACROSS

1	DESPISED
4	SHORT; QUICK
6	CLOTHING WORN WHILE CARRYING AN UMBRELLA
8	CALMED A WILD ANIMAL
9	MAKE A HOLE IN THE DIRT
11	GRILLED SLICE OF BEEF
13	TO PLACE SILVERWARE ON A DINNER TABLE
15	RISE TO YOUR FEET
17	LAND TURTLE
18	NOT DEAD
19	PART OF BODY BETWEEN NECK AND ABDOMEN

DOWN

1	OPPOSITE OF FIRED
2	OBJECT; ENTITY
3	RESPECTABLE
4	VESSEL FOR TRAVELING ON WATER
5	OPPOSITE OF INCOME
7	SHORT, STUBBY NAIL; THUMB _____
10	TO CONNECT AN APPLIANCE (EXAMPLE: DISHWASHER)
11	MAILED A LETTER
12	POLAR BEARS LIVE HERE, AROUND THE NORTH POLE
13	CINNAMON, NUTMEG, AND PEPPER ARE EXAMPLES OF THIS
14	HALLOWEEN ALTERNATIVE TO TRICK
16	COOING BIRD

CROSSWORD PUZZLE 5

DRAW TOPPINGS FOR THE ICE CREAM.

–

ANSWER KEY

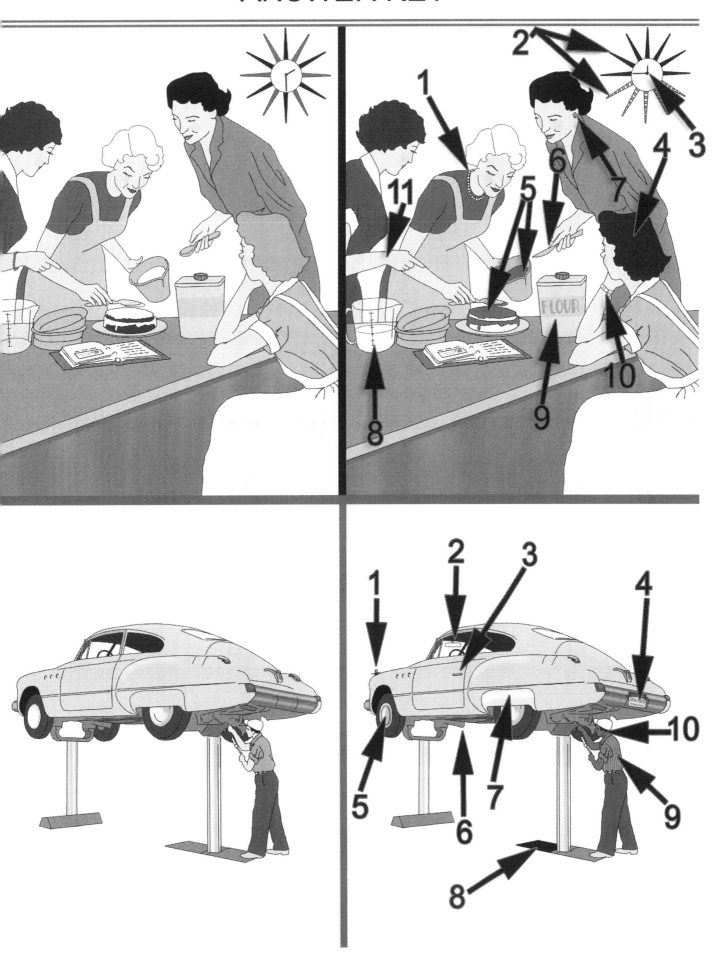

CROSSWORD PUZZLE ANSWERS

PUZZLE 1

COFFEETABLE · SAD · DEAR · THAT · OUR
POSTER · THUG
FUND · SINGER
HEN · SAD
MOTHER · OUT
NET · COOING

PUZZLE 2

FATHER · DROP
WOOD · EDIBLE
NOSY · SEND
ACTIVE · SONG
CAVE · SILVER

PUZZLE 3

SNORE · BROTH
PUDDLE · DEAF
EGG · BROWNIE
BICYCLE · LAW
ROOF · BUBBLE
PANTS · STOOL

PUZZLE 4

GRAPE · CLASS
RECESSION
CURVE · TEARS · END
BAT · EXTROVERT
HOMER · EARLY

PUZZLE 5

HATED · BRIEF
RAINCOAT
TAMED
DIG · STEAK
STAND · SET
TORTOISE
ALIVE · CHEST

ANSWER KEY

CARS

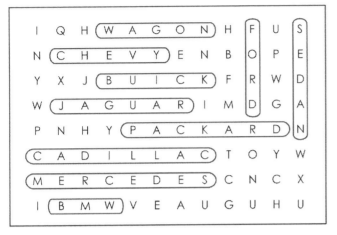

COLORS

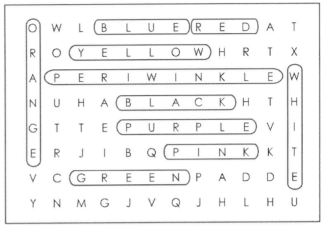

FIREFIGHTER

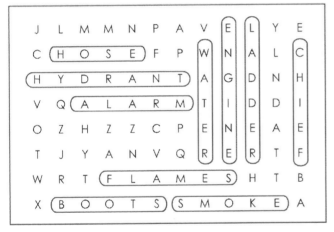

FOODS

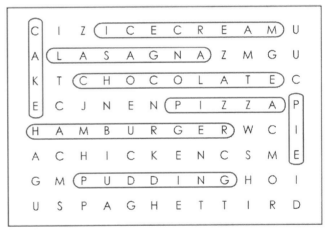

ICE CREAM

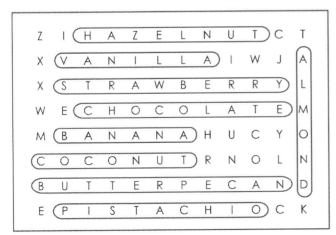

MOVIE STARS

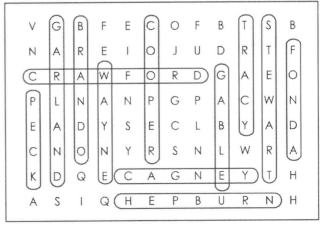

ANSWER KEY

MUSICAL INSTRUMENTS

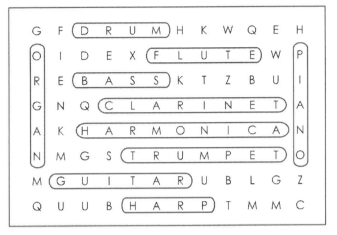

PRESIDENTS

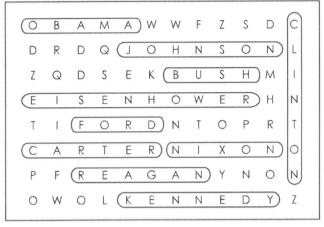

SPRING

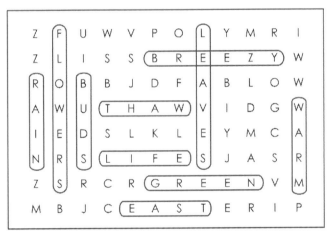

RELIGION

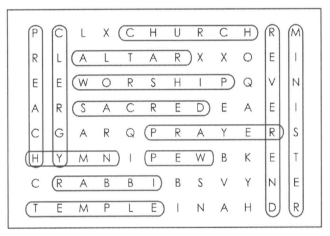

BOOZE

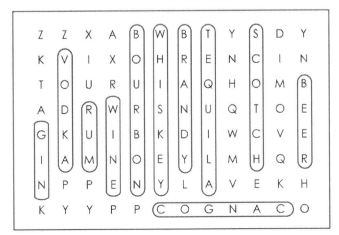

THE FLU

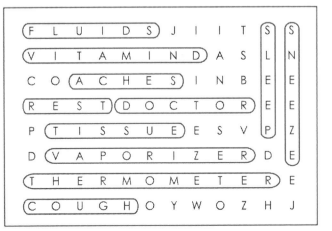

ANSWER KEY

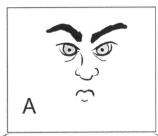

A

I've been waiting for this parking spot for a long time-- that young guy is not going to steal it from me. 1

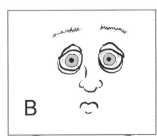

B

I cheated on my taxes and now I'm being audited.... 3

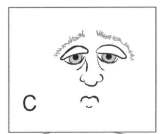

C

I can't believe I ate the whole thing. 2

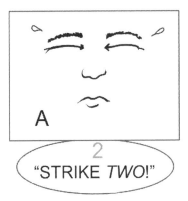

A

2 "STRIKE *TWO!*"

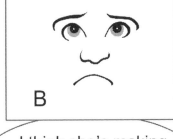

B

I think she's making fun of my bald head.... 1

C

If she thinks she's going to cut this line and get in front of me, she's crazy.... 3

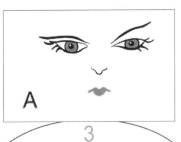

A

3 Do you really expect me to finish this work by myself?

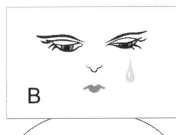

B

I think they forgot my birthday.... 1

C

Hey, handsome! 2

ANSWER KEY

—

ANSWER KEY

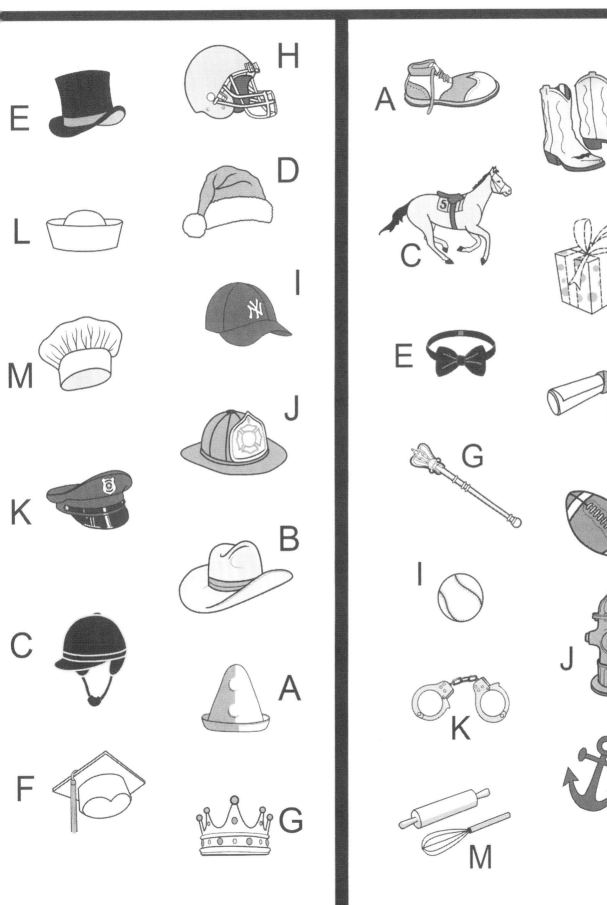

I HOPE YOU FOUND
FUN INSIDE
THIS BOOK!

I WOULD GREATLY APPRECIATE HEARING FROM YOU!
WHICH ACTIVITIES DID YOU ENJOY?
ARE THERE ANY THAT WERE NOT FUN FOR YOU TO DO?

PLEASE TELL ME YOUR THOUGHTS AND SUGGESTIONS!
DIANE@LIFEENHANCER.EXPERT

Made in the USA
Middletown, DE
14 November 2020